7 7/22 ᵤ 7/18

AMERICA'S INDUSTRIAL SOCIETY IN THE 19TH CENTURY ™

Railroads and Steamships

Important Developments in American Transportation

Suzanne J. Murdico

rosen central

Primary Source™

The Rosen Publishing Group, Inc., New York

For Brian Plante

Published in 2004 by The Rosen Publishing Group, Inc.
29 East 21st Street, New York, NY 10010

First Edition

Library of Congress Cataloging-in-Publication Data

Murdico, Suzanne J.
Railroads and steamships: important developments in American transportation/by Suzanne J. Murdico.—1st ed.
    v. cm.—(America's industrial society in the 19th century)
Includes bibliographical references and index.
Contents: A growing need for transportation—The Iron Horse and the *Clermont*—Railroads: joining east and west—Steamships: gateway to the world.
ISBN 0-8239-4024-1 (library binding)
ISBN 0-8239-4278-3 (paperback)
6-pack ISBN 0-8239-4290-2
1. Railroads—United States—History—19th century—Juvenile literature. 2. Steamboats—United States—History—19th century—Juvenile literature. [1. Railroads—History—19th century. 2. Steamboats—History—19th century. 3. Transportation—History.]
I. Title. II. Series.
HE2751 .M87 2004
385'.0973'09034—dc21

2002155514

Manufactured in the United States of America

On the cover: large images: Civil War-era steam locomotive; steamship *Ben Campbell* at dockside. First row (from left to right): steamship docked at a landing; Tammany Hall on election night, 1859; map showing U.S. railroad routes in 1883; detail of bank note, 1822, Bank of the Commonwealth of Kentucky; People's Party (Populist) Convention at Columbus, Nebraska, 1890; Republican ticket, 1865. Second row: William McKinley gives a campaign speech in 1896; parade banner of the Veterans of the Haymarket Riot; Alexander Graham Bell's sketch of the telephone, c. 1876; public declaration on how government can crush monopolies; city planners' illustration of Stockton, California; railroad construction camp, Nebraska, 1889.

Photo credits: cover top right and left © Library of Congress, Prints and Photographs Division; p. 5 © Smithsonian American Art Museum, Washington DC/Art Resource, NY; pp. 7, 13 © Hulton/Archive/Getty Images; p. 10 © Bettmann/Corbis; pp. 12, 16 © Library of Congress, Geography and Map Division; p. 14 © Archivo Iconografico, S.A./Corbis; p. 17 © Library of Congress; p. 19 © Central Pacific Railroad Photographic History Museum; p. 22 © Mystic Seaport; p. 23 © Culver Pictures Inc.; p. 25 © Mansell/Timepix.

Designer: Tahara Hasan; **Editor:** Mark Beyer; **Photo Researcher:** Peter Tomlinson

Contents

1
A Growing Need
for Transportation

Before the 1800s, Americans didn't have much need for long-distance transportation. The United States was an agricultural society. Most families had their own farms. They lived off of the land, raising crops and livestock. They also made most of their own clothing and furniture by hand. Sometimes they used simple machines. Any other items that they needed could usually be bought locally. People already had what they needed to live. So they didn't really need to travel to far-off places. They also didn't need to buy goods from other areas.

The development of industrialization changed all that. In the early 1800s, the Industrial Revolution caused a huge increase in the production of goods. Inventions such as the steam engine brought power-driven machinery into use. These machines helped create the business of mass

Many Americans lived on farms throughout the 1800s. They harvested grains, fruits, and vegetables for sale at town markets. For the country to grow, farms needed railroads to carry their products to city markets. Once railroads connected rural and urban areas, farms and cities were able to grow. The increased food supply helped America grow, too.

production of goods. With mass production, goods can be made much faster and cheaper than by hand. Mass production requires large machines and many workers to operate them. So manufacturing moved out of homes and into factories. Most factories were located in large cities.

This increase in the production of goods created a growing need for transportation. Some of this transportation would take place over great distances. Workers needed raw materials in order to manufacture the goods. Cotton and wood are examples of raw materials. These raw materials had to be transported to the factories. After the products were made

The Age of Steam

The idea behind the steam engine is pretty simple. Think about the steam that escapes from a boiling teakettle or a heated iron used to press clothes. When water is heated to its boiling point, it turns into steam. Steam kept under pressure builds up and creates great power. Steam power could push a wheel system that made trains move. Great steam locomotives could carry many more tons of goods at faster speeds than horse and carriage.

England was the first country to use steam locomotives, in 1825. Soon after, the United States and other countries used steam trains. Steam power was also used to move boats and ships. Early steamboats traveled the inland rivers and other waterways within the United States.

These diagrams show figures of Watt's steam engine (s119–122) and Hornblower's steam engine (s123–125). The improved uses of steam power made mechanized factories possible. Factories drew people from farm life to city life. America was now able to make products for sale around the world. These included cloth, machine tools, and home-use products.

using the raw materials, they needed to be moved. The products would be taken to marketplaces around the country and the world. There, they would be sold.

There were some problems, however. One major problem involved the types of transportation used. Cars,

trucks, and airplanes had not yet been invented. So trains and ships were used to move people and goods. But at the time, these forms of transportation were not very fast or trustworthy. They also couldn't easily travel long distances. The other major problem was that the networks of rail lines, roads, and waterways could not meet the growing transportation needs of the Industrial Revolution. These networks would have to be improved and expanded. They needed to stretch from coast to coast. Transportation routes had to connect cities.

Important improvements were soon to come in both transportation and networks. Advances in railroads and shipping would greatly help the growth of industrialization. In 1840, manufacturing made up less than 20 percent of all production in the United States. Just 20 years later, this number had grown to more than 30 percent. By the end of the century, manufacturing was a vital part of the U.S. economy. The United States had changed into the most powerful industrial nation in the world. Growth in transportation helped to make that success possible.

2

The Iron Horse and the *Clermont*

In the early 1800s, most people traveled by foot or horse-drawn carriage. For longer trips, horse-drawn trains could carry several people at once. These trains weren't a very fast way to travel. They also weren't all that comfortable. But they did get people where they wanted to go. During the Industrial Revolution, however, a new invention would replace the horse-drawn train. That invention was the steam locomotive. Locomotives pull or push trains along railroad tracks.

A locomotive needs fuel to run. In steam locomotives, coal or fuel oil is burned to create heat. This heat is then applied to water in the locomotive's boiler, which produces steam. The pressure of the steam is used to move the locomotive's wheels.

The trainbuilder Peter Cooper raced a horse-drawn train in his steam locomotive Tom Thumb in 1830. The horse-drawn train won the race when Tom Thumb's engine broke down. The race proved that steam-powered locomotives were the future of travel.

Peter Cooper built an early steam locomotive called the Tom Thumb. (Tom Thumb was the name of a famous circus performer.) Cooper wanted to prove that his locomotive could travel faster than a horse-drawn train. So he set down a challenge to officials of the Baltimore and Ohio Railroad. A race was held on August 28, 1830. It

was between the railroad's horse-drawn train and Cooper's steam locomotive. The Tom Thumb was leading the race before it developed engine problems. The horse-drawn train won the race. This was only the beginning for the steam locomotive, or "iron horse."

At the end of 1830, steam locomotives were put into regular use in the United States. They carried both people and freight. Steam locomotives quickly became popular. They became common transportation for people. Locomotives did have problems, however. The locomotive's fire must constantly be fed in order to produce the steam needed to keep the engine running. A great deal of fuel must be burned to produce power. Much of the heat created, though, is wasted.

In the late 1800s, the electric locomotive was developed. In 1895, the Baltimore and Ohio Railroad began placing electric locomotives in regular service. The iron horse remained the more popular choice. American railroads used steam locomotives through the end of the 1800s and into the following century.

Locomotives weren't the only way to travel during the Industrial Revolution. For some trips, water was a better choice than rail. At first, riverboats were used to move goods over water. Goods could be easily floated downstream on flatboats. The trip upstream was a different story. The boats

By 1840, the Baltimore and Ohio Railroad company connected hundreds of towns and cities in the United States. Roadway trade routes now connected to rail lines. Railroad service helped states more easily do business with each other. The Industrial Revolution was by now in full motion. The country's wealth grew, and people began to earn better wages.

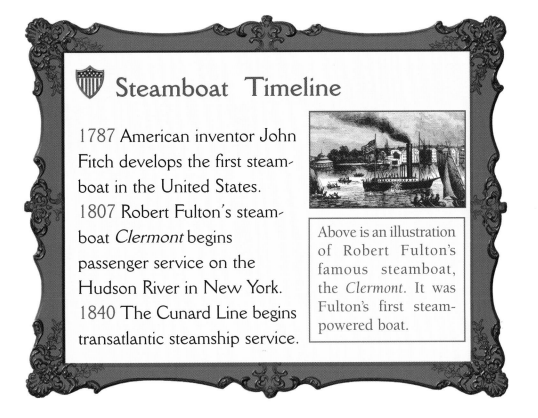

Steamboat Timeline

1787 American inventor John Fitch develops the first steamboat in the United States.
1807 Robert Fulton's steamboat *Clermont* begins passenger service on the Hudson River in New York.
1840 The Cunard Line begins transatlantic steamship service.

Above is an illustration of Robert Fulton's famous steamboat, the *Clermont*. It was Fulton's first steam-powered boat.

needed power to travel upstream against the current. Inventors realized that boats could also be powered by steam.

American Robert Fulton didn't invent the steamboat. He was the first person to build a steamboat used to make money. In 1807, Fulton's *Clermont* began passenger service between New York City and Albany, New York. The boat had large paddle wheels powered by steam. It traveled at the speed of 5 miles per hour. This meant that the 150-mile trip up the Hudson River took 30 hours. Compared with today's

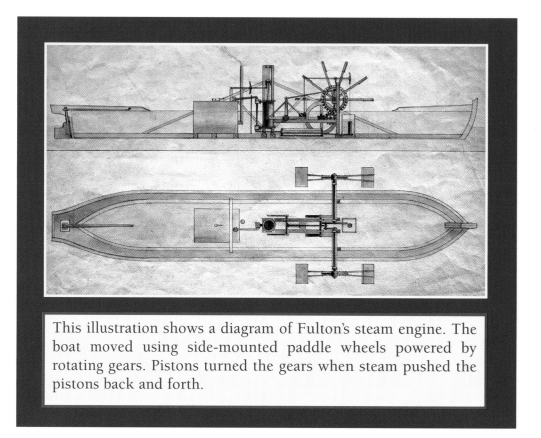

This illustration shows a diagram of Fulton's steam engine. The boat moved using side-mounted paddle wheels powered by rotating gears. Pistons turned the gears when steam pushed the pistons back and forth.

travel, that sounds really slow. For the early 1800s, the *Clermont* was faster than other forms of transportation.

Within a few years, steamboats could be seen often. They traveled the rivers and other inland waterways of the eastern United States. Within 10 years, steamboats traveled on waterways as far west as the Mississippi River. Soon after, larger steamboats headed out to sea. They carried both goods and passengers to and from other countries of the world.

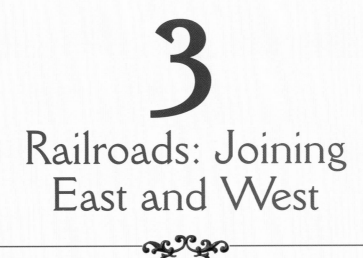

Railroads: Joining East and West

The Industrial Revolution was quickly creating a demand for railroads. By the mid-1800s, railroad construction in the northeastern United States was well under way. Rail lines usually connected two cities near each other. For example, railroads linked New York City with New Haven, Connecticut. Other rail lines joined Washington, D.C., with Richmond, Virginia. By 1850, railroad companies had built 9,000 miles of railroad track in the eastern United States.

There was still a growing need for rail lines to reach the Midwest. During the 1850s, four major railroads were built to connect cities in the Northeast with the Great Lakes. These railroads included the Erie Railroad, the Pennsylvania Railroad, the Baltimore and Ohio (B&O) Railroad, and the New York Central Railroad. Now freight

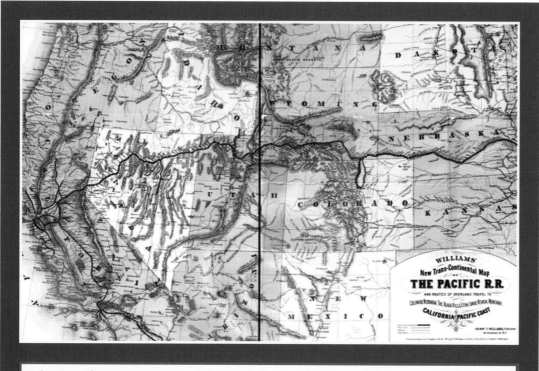

The Pacific Railroad Act mapped the route from the West Coast to the Midwest before starting the transcontinental railroad. This map shows cities and towns along the route. The Union Pacific and Central Pacific railroad tracks met in Utah in 1869. This finally connected the rail tracks of the eastern and western United States.

could travel easily between the East Coast and the Great Lakes. The Mississippi River was also an important trade route. So rail lines were built to connect it with the city of Chicago. Soon after, rail lines reached to St. Louis on the Mississippi River.

By this time, rail lines were also being built to link cities in the Southeast. By 1860, more than 30,000 miles of railroad track had been completed in the United States. But much of the western part of the country remained a wild frontier. During the first half of the 1800s, many animals,

Train service carried people and merchandise through every landscape in America. Train travel through the western deserts was much safer than traveling by horse-drawn wagon. Notice the Native Americans standing on the ridge overlooking the passing train.

but not many people, lived in the West. There was no easy way for people or goods to get there by land. The journey from east to west was long and difficult. It also involved traveling across large mountain ranges.

By the early 1860s, the U.S. government saw the need to extend transportation to the West Coast. The solution was to build a transcontinental railroad. This railroad would allow trains to travel all the way across the North American continent. The rail lines were already finished from the East Coast to the Mississippi River. So the new lines would be joined with the existing lines. This would extend the railroad all the way to California.

In 1862, the U.S. Congress passed the Pacific Railroad Act. The task of building the new railroad was given to the Central Pacific Railroad and the Union Pacific Railroad. In 1863, the Central Pacific began work on its section. The track started in Sacramento, California, and moved east. In 1865, work began on the Union Pacific track. It started near Omaha, Nebraska, and headed west toward Sacramento.

Building this railroad was very difficult and dangerous. The track had to cross two huge mountain ranges—the Rockies and the Sierra Nevada. It would also cross the Nevada desert. To complete this giant task, the Central Pacific

A painting from around 1881 shows the golden spike ceremony at Promontory Point, Utah, in 1869. Railroad executives from both the Central Pacific and Union Pacific companies came to the final spike ceremony. California governor Leland Stanford hit the head of a ceremonial gold spike. That spike can now be seen in the Stanford Museum, Stanford, CA.

hired thousands of Chinese immigrants. Thousands of European immigrants worked on building the Union Pacific side of the railroad.

The Central Pacific and the Union Pacific tracks finally met on May 10, 1869. The place was Promontory Point,

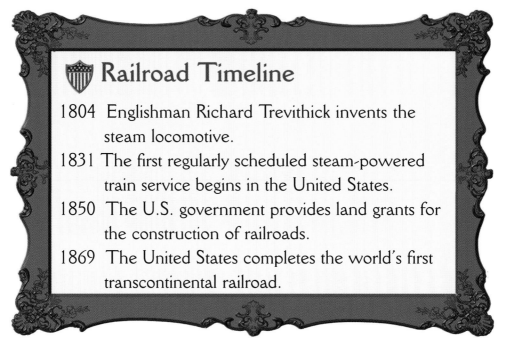

Railroad Timeline

1804 Englishman Richard Trevithick invents the steam locomotive.

1831 The first regularly scheduled steam-powered train service begins in the United States.

1850 The U.S. government provides land grants for the construction of railroads.

1869 The United States completes the world's first transcontinental railroad.

Utah. The joining of these two rail lines was a special moment for the United States. Celebrations and ceremonies marked the event. North America had become the first continent to have a transcontinental railroad. The western United States could now be settled. Goods could be traded from coast to coast. The country was now able to grow larger and faster than ever before.

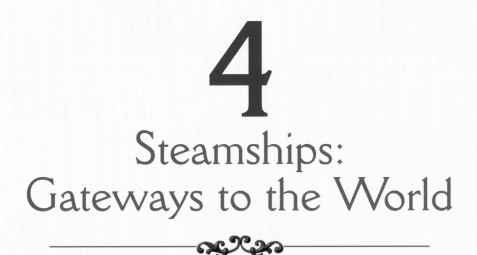

4

Steamships: Gateways to the World

Steamboats had become a common means of transportation during the 1800s. They carried people and goods to cities and towns within North America. These were mostly short trips on calm waters. What about people and goods that needed to travel across the ocean to Europe or other places? How did they travel?

Before the 1800s, transatlantic passengers traveled by sailing ship. In those days, crossing the Atlantic Ocean was a risky voyage. The trip was long, difficult, and uncomfortable. Relying on the wind to propel the sails meant a rocky and dangerous journey. Most people didn't want to make such a trip.

At first, it was unclear whether the steam engine could be used to power a large ship. One problem was the huge amount of fuel required. Would the ship have enough

Steamboats traveled up and down the Ohio River at regular times throughout the year. Merchandise moving from city to city helped the country to grow quickly. Factories sprang up in the late nineteenth century to help towns—and their people—prosper in the manufacturing business.

steam to make it all the way across the ocean? Also, a ship with a large engine had yet to be tested on the open sea. How would it handle the rough waves?

In 1819, an American ship proved that this trip could be done. The *Savannah* became the first steamship to cross the Atlantic Ocean. This ship didn't rely only on steam, though. It was equipped with sails in case of engine problems or a fuel shortage. In 1827, the *Curacao* became the

first ship to make the transatlantic voyage powered only by steam. Even so, the trip took an entire month!

Soon, though, more and more steamships started crossing the Atlantic. The trip became faster and faster, too. In 1840, British shipowner Samuel Cunard began the first regular transatlantic steamship service. The Cunard Line started out carrying mail and then moved on to passenger service. The Cunard company is still in business today.

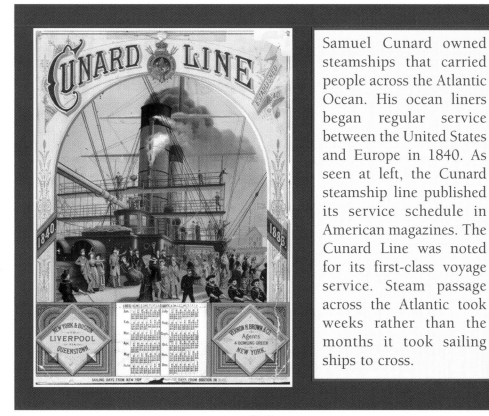

Samuel Cunard owned steamships that carried people across the Atlantic Ocean. His ocean liners began regular service between the United States and Europe in 1840. As seen at left, the Cunard steamship line published its service schedule in American magazines. The Cunard Line was noted for its first-class voyage service. Steam passage across the Atlantic took weeks rather than the months it took sailing ships to cross.

The development of steamships was a huge step forward for the Industrial Revolution. Just as railroads joined the eastern and western United States, steamships joined North America with other continents. Goods from U.S. manufacturers could now be shipped and sold to other

The *Titanic*

The most famous steamship in history is probably the *Titanic*. It was a British luxury passenger liner built in the early 1900s. At that time, it was the largest and most deluxe ship on the ocean. The *Titanic* was also considered so safe as to be unsinkable. That idea was proven wrong, though, on the ship's very first voyage.

The *Titanic* was headed to New York City from Southampton, England. On the night of April 14, 1912, the great ship hit an iceberg in the North Atlantic Ocean. The impact caused the ship's seams to buckle and allow water to enter. Within a few hours, the mighty *Titanic* sank into the icy waters. No one had thought that the ship could sink. So it was not equipped with enough lifeboats for all the passengers. About 1,500 people lost their lives.

By the early twentieth century, ocean steamship travel was at its height of popularity. Huge ships carrying hundreds of people steamed across the North Atlantic every week. Above is a photo of the *Titanic* leaving Belfast, Ireland, on its first, and last, transatlantic journey in April 1912.

countries. Opening up this huge market allowed manufacturers to produce and sell more goods. Being able to transport goods quickly and reliably also saved money for manufacturers. These advantages allowed U.S. companies to earn higher profits.

The advent of steamships also helped to change the face of the U.S. population. People could now travel easily and quickly between North America and other continents. This led to millions of people from European countries moving to the United States. The 1800s saw a huge increase in the U.S. population. Many people came to start new lives. They often lived in cities and worked in factories.

By the end of the 1800s, steamships had replaced sailing ships. Steamships transported people and goods all over the world. Until the invention of the airplane in the twentieth century, steamships remained the fastest way to travel across the ocean.

Glossary

agricultural (a-grih-KUL-chuh-rul)   Referring to the raising of crops and farm animals; farming.

economy (ih-KAH-nuh-mee)   The management of money and resources.

factories (FAK-tuh-reez)   Buildings where goods are manufactured.

freight (FRAYT)   Goods that are transported from one place to another.

frontier (frun-TEER)   Area of a country that has not yet been settled.

immigrants (IH-muh-grintz)   People who move to a different country to live.

industrialization (in-DUS-tree-ul-ehz-a-shun)   The development of industries as a vital part of a country's economy.

inland (IN-land)   Located far from the coast or border.

livestock (LYV-stok)   Farm animals, such as horses and cows.

locomotive (**loh-kuh-MOH-tiv**)   An engine that pulls or pushes trains along railroad tracks.

manufacturing (**man-yuh-FAK-cher-ing**)   Making goods by hand or by machine.

mass production (**MAS pruh-DUK-shun**)   The manufacturing of goods in large quantities.

population (**pop-yoo-LAY-shun**)   The people who live in a particular area.

profits (**PRAH-fits**)   Money earned by a business.

raw materials (**RAW muh-TEER-ee-uhlz**)   Items used to make finished goods.

transatlantic (**tranz-at-LAN-tic**)   Across the Atlantic Ocean.

transcontinental (**tranz-kon-tin-EN-tul**)   Across a continent, such as North America.

transportation (**tranz-per-TAY-shun**)   The action of carrying people or goods from one place to another.

Web Sites

Due to the changing nature of Internet links, the Rosen Publishing Group, Inc., has developed an online list of Web sites related to the subject of this book. This site is updated regularly. Please use this link to access the list:

http://www.rosenlinks.com/aistc/rast

Primary Source Image List

Page 5: Oil painting, *October,* by John Whetten Ehninger, 1867. Currently housed at the Smithsonian American Art Museum, Washington, D.C.

Page 7: Diagram of Watt's improved steam engine and Hornblower's steam engine, circa 1816.

Page 10: Nineteenth-century color illustration of 1830 race between the Tom Thumb locomotive and a B&O horse-drawn train.

Page 12: Map of the Baltimore & Ohio Railroad connecting lines, 1860. Currently housed at the Library of Congress, Washington, D.C.

Page 13: Illustration of Robert Fulton's first steamboat, *Clermont,* 1807.

Page 14: Robert Fulton's diagram for steam propulsion, circa eighteenth century.

Page 16: Map of Pacific Railroad routes through American West, 1877. Currently housed at the Library of Congress, Washington, D.C.

Page 17: Photograph of the Jupiter train carrying railway officials to golden spike ceremony, 1869. Currently housed at the Library of Congress, Washington, D.C.

Page 19: Oil painting *The Last Spike,* 1881, by Thomas Hill. Currently housed at the California State Railroad Museum, Sacramento, CA.

Page 22: Photograph of a steamboat on the Ohio River, circa 1890. Currently housed at the Mystic Seaport Museum, Mystic, Connecticut.

Page 23: Magazine advertisement for Cunard shipping line schedule, 1883.

Page 25: Photograph of the steamship *Titanic* leaving Belfast, Ireland, 1912.

Index

About the Author

Suzanne J. Murdico is a freelance writer who has authored numerous books for children and teens. She lives in Florida with her husband, Vinnie, and their cat, Zuzu.